THE SUPERNATURAL MINISTRY OF
ANGELS

guardian

I0150433

defense

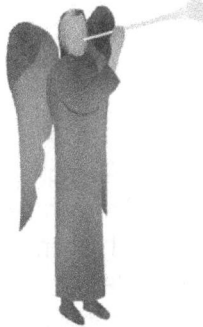

message

enthusiasm

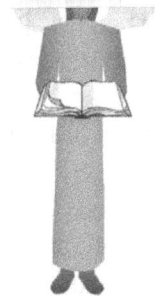

word

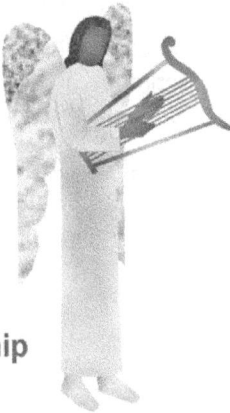

worship

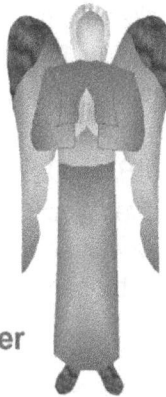

prayer

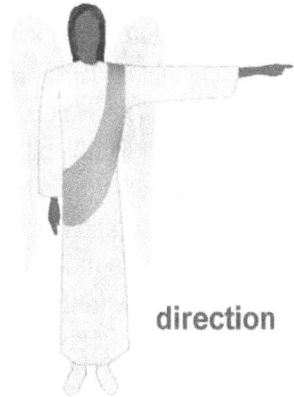

direction

by
David A. Castro

The Supernatural Ministry of Angels

Printed in the United States of America

International Standard Book Number: 0-9637001-7-0

GENERAL LISTING OF ANGELIC ORDERS AND EMPLOYMENTS

Angel of the Lord: Jesus' angel or Jesus Himself, God's Messenger; dispatched one; Gabriel, the chief messenger of divine revelations; prophet, priest or king; ambassador; Hebrew: *malak;* Malachi 3:1

Archangel: first or beginning chief, Michael; Greek: *archaggelos;* Jude 9

Heavenly hosts: an army of soldiers spread out across a large area; Hebrew: *tsebaah;* Greek: *stratia;* Luke 2:13

Innumerable company of angels: a myriad of messengers; Greek: *murias, aggelos;* Hebrews 12:22

Cherubim: divine figures called the Living Creatures, guardians of the Shekinah Glory of God; Hebrew: *keruwb;* Genesis 3:24, Ezekiel 10:15

Seraphim: fiery ones, burners; Hebrew: *saraph;* Isaiah 6:1-3

Angels of the Churches (stars): messengers, ministers, pastors; Greek: *aggelos;* Revelation 1:20

Thrones: potentates; Greek: *thronos;* Colossians 1:16

Dominions: controllers, governors, rulers, masters, lords; Greek: *kuriotes;* Colossians 1:16

Principalities: chief magistrates; Greek: *arche;* Colossians 1:16

Powers: authorities, superhuman ones with jurisdiction, privilege and liberty; Greek: *exousia;* Colossians 1:16

Dignities: glorious ones, praisers, worshipers; Greek: *doxa;* 2Peter 2:10

Mights: powerful ones, able ones, miraculous ones; Greek: *dunamai;* Ephesians 1:21

Spirits: winds, tempests, storms, whirlwinds, air, breath, life, soul, inspirational thoughts; Hebrew: *ruwach;* Greek: *pneuma;* Psalms 104:4

Chariots: riders on vehicles, troops, soldiers, cavalry; Hebrew: *rekeb;* Psalms 68:17

Wings of the wind: edges, ends, borders, corners, feathers; Hebrew: *kanaph;* Psalms 18:10

Ministering spirits: attendants, waiters, servers, givers, obeyers; Greek: *leitourgikos;* Hebrews 1:14

Watchers: guardian angels, seers, recorders; Hebrew: *iyr;* Daniel 4:13

Legions: regiments of soldiers; Greek: *legeon;* Matthew 26:53

Men: angels as regular fellows, albeit in shining garments; Greek: *aner;* Luke 24:4

Strangers: angels as guests, foreigners; Greek: *philonexia;* Hebrews 13:2

Birds: winged fliers; Hebrew: *owph;* Ecclesiastes 10:20

TABLE OF CONTENTS

Chapter 1: A PROPHECY

"There is coming a visitation of angels, saith the Spirit of Grace. There is coming a manifestation of My power and My anointing in these last days which has not been in times past. You are on the verge of the greatest visitation of the Spirit of God that has ever come to earth. Give the more earnest heed unto the things which you have heard about supernatural manifestations, and give the more earnest heed unto the things which you have heard about miracles, and give the more earnest heed unto the things which you have heard about visions, and give the more earnest heed unto the things which you have heard about angels. For there is coming in this last hour of the Age a demonstration of My power by angelic administration, saith the Lord of hosts. Learn of them, that ye may cooperate with them, that ye may discern them, that ye may receive and not grieve them at their visitation. But yet take heed in these areas, for the spirit of error doth work, and Satan has, at times, transformed himself into an angel of light. But know Me, know My Word, know My Spirit, and I will guide thee by My light, and you shall know My leading, and you shall know My manifestation, and you shall know the angel of My presence.

"My angels will protect you from harm, even as in the time of David, when he was being persecuted by Saul and was consistently rescued. At times, they will speak to you and cause you to understand the interpretations of the revelations which I would disclose unto you, even as in the time of Daniel, when My angel appeared unto him and showed him things which were yet to come. They will assist you in your finances, in your relationships and in your general well-being. They will help you to preach and minister in the salvation of souls, because they are serving spirits which I have sent forth to minister for them who shall be heirs of salvation. They will also, at times, manifest themselves unto you visibly and give you discernment concerning many things

and people. At times, they will whisper, and your ears will hear a word behind you, saying, "This is the way, walk ye in it," as My angel will order your goings.

"And so hear ye, and take ye heed to what I have said in My Word concerning the ministry of the angels, and you will be blessed, and you will prosper, and you will know My will, and you will be delivered from harm. For the Lord thy God doth love thee, and hath given unto thee an inheritance with the saints in light, and hath dispatched for thy service the fellow-servants of thy brethren the prophets before thee, and will keep thee in the hour of temptation by them. Thus saith the Lord of hosts."

(Prophetic word of the Lord given by David A. Castro, May 1988.)

Chapter 2: KINDS OF ANGELS

Judges 13:18-19 (amp) And the Angel of the Lord said to him, Why do you ask My name, seeing it is wonderful? [Isaiah 9:6] So Manoah took the kid with the cereal offering, and offered it upon a rock to the Lord, the Angel working wonders, while Manoah and his wife looked on.

Our God is a God of signs and wonders. His Name in Isaiah 9:6, "Wonderful," (Hebrew: *peleh*) means "Full of wonders." Here, in the context of Judges 13, we see an angel of the Lord also named "Wonderful," and also working wonders. Angels of God are directly involved in, and often responsible for, supernatural signs and wonders.

There are a great many different kinds of angels: cherubims (Ezekiel 10:5), seraphims (Isaiah 6:2), warriors (Daniel 10:13), messengers (Daniel 10:14), and others. They have many ranks and many duties. Some are stationed in the heavens, some around the earth; some are always before the Throne of God in the Third Heaven, and some are employed in ministering to God's people on earth.

Some angels are especially equipped to demonstrate supernatural powers. Many of the supernatural experiences that are recorded in the Bible came by an angelic manifestation of some sort. They are not always specifically identified or acknowledged as the causator, but they always partake in supernatural demonstrations in some way.

In changing the weather, controlling the elements, and ordering natural events; in healings, miracles, and manifestations of the Holy Ghost with fire; in prophecies, visions, and falling out under the power of God; in the leadings of the Holy Spirit of God, even to the subtlest of whispers and impressions; in all the works of the Lord, angels are actively involved.

In several trances from the Lord which I have experienced, I have seen angels ministering for me in some capacity. I would either see them doing something in the realm of the spirit, or hear them giving me a message, or both. Still more profoundly, I have experienced them coming upon me suddenly—literally and physically—filling my body with theirs while my spirit would go out of my body. Then, when my spirit would come back, they would let go of me and lift off, just as suddenly as they came.

Perhaps the *hand of the Lord God* which *fell* upon Ezekiel (in Ezekiel 1:8) was an angel of the Lord sent to encamp (abide) round about his body while his spirit went flying through the Temple in Jerusalem. The spiritual flying experiences as well were assisted by angels with wings and also, occasionally, by supernatural vehicles:

Ezekiel 3:13 I heard also the noise of the wings of the living creatures that touched one another, and the noise of the wheels over against them, and a noise of a great rushing.

Psalms 68:17a   The *chariots of God* are twenty thousand, even thousands of angels.

The "noise" of the "wheels" of the "Chariots" (from the Hebrew word: *rekeb,* "vehicles, wagons") of God's angels suggests to us that there is in the invisible realm equipment and mechanical devices of a very high order which the angels use. Today we would call these "cars."

The Bible also shows that many supernatural demonstrations of fire were in fact angelic manifestations. The angel of the Lord appeared unto Moses in a flame of fire out of the midst of a bush:

Exodus 3:2   And the angel of the Lord appeared unto him in *a flame of fire* out of the midst of a bush: and he looked, and, behold, the bush burned with fire, and the bush was not consumed.

This same angel, or another angel of similar rank and anointing, became a pillar of fire (and also a pillar of cloud) in his ministry to the Israelites. Some verses identify the Lord as that fire:

Exodus 13:21   And *the Lord* went before them by day in a pillar of cloud, to lead them the way; and by night in a pillar of fire, to give them light; to go by day and night: He took not away the pillar of the cloud by day, nor the pillar of fire by night, from before the people.

And some verses identify an angel as being that fire:

Exodus 14:19   And *the angel* of God, which went before the camp of Israel, removed and went behind them; and the pillar of the cloud went from before their face, and stood behind them.

THE SUPERNATURAL MINISTRY OF ANGELS

The works of the Lord are sometimes attributed to Him, and at other times to His angels. It is written that God spoke to Moses on Mount Sinai:

Exodus 19:9a And the Lord said unto Moses, Lo, *I come* unto thee in a thick cloud, that the people may hear when I speak with thee, and believe thee forever.

And, again, the Word says that it was an angel of God that spoke to him there:

Acts 7:38 This is he, that was in the Church in the wilderness with the angel which spake to him in the Mount Sina, and with our fathers.

The actions of the Holy Ghost, too, in the Book of Acts, were not performed without the supernatural ministries, interventions, instructions, and guidance of angels. In the account of Philip, the Evangelist, when he was led to minister to the Ethiopian eunuch, the Bible says that he was instructed by an angel, and also by the Holy Spirit:

Acts 8:26 And the angel of the Lord spake unto Philip, saying, Arise, and go toward the south unto the way that goeth down from Jerusalem unto Gaza, which is desert.

Acts 8:29 Then the Spirit said unto Philip, Go near, and join thyself to this chariot.

Though we may not always see, hear, or sense them, angels of God, in one form or another, are involved in the supernatural experiences God gives us.

Hebrews 1:14 (amp) Are not the angels all (servants) ministering spirits, sent out in the service [of God for the assistance] of those who are to inherit salvation?

The angels are ministering spirits, serving spirits, sent forth by God to help those who will receive deliverance; that is, to help us if we are willing to receive deliverance. The word "salvation" (from the Greek: *soteria,* "deliverance") in this context signifies "rescue from temporal dangers, and assistance in temporal matters." It does not signify "redemption," which is "salvation of the soul by faith in Christ," (Ephesians 1:7). If it meant that, then the angels would only serve and help those who are, or who will become, Christians. But, as we shall see, Christians and non-Christians alike can receive help by the ministries of the angels.

Hebrews 2:1-3a (amp) Since all this is true, we ought to pay much closer attention than ever to the truths that we have heard, lest in any way we drift past [them] and slip away. For if the message given through angels [that is, the Law spoken by them to Moses] was authentic and proved sure, and every violation and disobedience received an appropriate (just and adequate) penalty, how shall we escape [appropriate retribution] if we neglect and refuse to pay attention to such a great salvation [as is now offered to us, letting it drift past us forever]?

Still referring to the help in the things of this life which the angels provide, this context declares that we should pay close attention, give earnest heed, to their ministries. The Spirit of God is saying, "Now concerning supernaturals, brethren, I would not have you to be ignorant," (1Corinthians 12:1). He is saying, "If ye be willing and obedient, ye shall partake of angelic assistance," (cf. Isaiah 1:19).

Now concerning the ministries of the angels, we should not be ignorant or negligent. We should be mindful of and obedient to the knowledge which has been given us about angels. Because if the ministry of angels in the time of the Patriarch Moses provided penalties for transgressors of the Law under the Old Covenant, how can we, today, escape dangers and problems if we cross the angels under the New Covenant, which is a better and more excellent administration?

They don't always let us know it, but the angels are always around and observing us; they also take notes on what we do, both good and bad, (Acts 10:4). Our problems may be caused by some displeasure we've given our angels. There are penalties for transgressors of God's laws, and God's people today, as the Israelites in the Old Testament, are not exempt from those penalties.

We cannot escape God's eternal judgments if we neglect so great a deliverance as He has provided for us in Christ's angels. In Hebrews 1-2, to show their involvement in the covenants of God, there are many references to the ministries of the angels: their relationship to Christ, their service to man, and our need to attend to the truths concerning them.

More facts from the Bible about angels

Angels are highly organized and extremely efficient in all their business, including:

a) in their presenting themselves before the Lord:

Job 1:6 Now there was a day when the sons of God came to present themselves before the Lord, and Satan came also among them.

b) in their order of worship:

Isaiah 6:1-3 In the year that King Uzziah died I saw also the Lord sitting upon a throne, high and lifted up, and His train filled the temple. Above it stood the seraphims: each one had six wings; with twain he covered his face, and with twain he covered his feet, and with twain he did fly. And one cried unto another, and said, Holy, holy, holy, is the Lord of hosts: the whole earth is full of His glory.

c) in ascending and descending between Heaven and earth:

Genesis 28:12 He dreamed, and behold a ladder set up on the earth, and the top of it reached to Heaven: and behold the angels of God ascending and descending on it.

 Angels have ranks:

Ephesians 1:20-21 (amp) Which He exerted in Christ when He raised Him from the dead and seated Him at His [own] right hand in the heavenly [places], Far above all *rule* and *authority* and *power* and *dominion,* and every name that is named—above *every title* that can be conferred—not only in this age and in this world, but also in the age and the world which are to come.

 Angels have names and titles:

Jude 9 Yet *Michael* the *archangel...*

 Angels are unlimited in number:

Hebrews 12:22 But ye are come unto Mount Sion, and unto the city of the Living God, the Heavenly Jerusalem, and to an *innumerable company* of angels.

Angels can appear in a variety of forms:

Hebrews 13:2 Be not forgetful to entertain *strangers:* for thereby some have entertained angels unawares.

Angels are preoccupied in the things concerning the Gospel of the Lord Jesus Christ:

1Peter 1:12 Unto whom it was revealed, that not unto themselves, but unto us they did minister the things, which are now reported unto you by them that have preached the Gospel unto you with the Holy Ghost sent down from Heaven; *which things the angels desire to look into.*

Angels, in everything that they do, always give Jesus Christ all the glory, honor, and praise:

Revelation 5:11-12 And I beheld, and I heard the voice of many angels round about the throne and the beasts and the elders: and the number of them was ten thousand times ten thousand, and thousands of thousands; Saying with a loud voice, *Worthy is the Lamb* that was slain to receive power, and riches, and wisdom, and strength, and honour, and glory, and blessing.

Chapter 3: JESUS, LORD OF ANGELS

Colossians 1:16-18   For by Him were all things created, that are in Heaven, and that are in earth, visible and invisible, whether they be thrones, or dominions, or principalities, or powers: all things were created by Him, and for Him: And He is before all things, and by Him all things consist. And He is the Head of the Body, the Church: Who is the Beginning, the Firstborn from the dead; that in all things He might have the preeminence.

Jesus Christ, the Head of the Church, created all things, including the invisible angelic hosts. Here, the angels are called thrones, dominions, principalities, and powers. There are many other titles by which they may be identified, but they are not all given in the Bible. Remember, God created an innumerable amount of angels and, we may suppose, He is still creating angels as needed.

In all things, Jesus is first in rank (preeminent) above all angels, and by Him all things consist ("cohere, are held together"). The worlds were framed by Jesus, the Word of God (Hebrews 11:3), and the angels, which assisted in the creation of the material universe and still do whatever He says, cause things to work together for our good (Romans 8:28), by hearkening unto—always hearing and obeying—the voice of the Word of God.

As we shall see in Chapter 9, we, too, can frame our own world and cause it to be held together and not come apart. As we speak the Word of God into our own lives and acknowledge the ministry of the angels, they will hearken unto the voice of the Word of God in our mouths, too. They will order aright the circumstances in our lives and cause them to work out for our good. The angels also back up, support, strengthen and affirm all our efforts to do good.

Psalms 103:20 Bless the Lord, ye His angels, that excel in strength, hearkening unto the voice of His Word.

God's Word in our mouths in a general way causes the angels to be involved in our lives in general ways. But when we voice God's Word with exactitude, they hearken unto that and serve and help us with meticulous precision.

Philippians 2:9-11 (tev) For this reason God raised Him to the highest place above and gave Him the Name that is greater than any other name. And so, in honor of the Name of Jesus all beings in Heaven, on earth, and in the world below will fall on their knees, and all will openly proclaim that Jesus Christ is Lord, to the glory of God the Father.

1Peter 3:22 Who is gone into Heaven, and is on the right hand of God; angels and authorities and powers being made subject unto Him.

Hebrews 1:6 And again, when He bringeth in the First Begotten into the world, He saith, And let all the angels of God worship Him.

All beings, even heavenly ones, must confess Jesus' lordship. All the angels, of whatever name or rank, worship Him and are made subject unto Him. Even though there are also evil angels, as we shall see in Chapter 7, even they, too, must bow the knee to the Name of Jesus and stop their strategies against us.

The good angels openly and willingly proclaim that Jesus Christ is Lord of all, and they do so to the glory of God the Father. The evil angels do so reluctantly, however, because they have been defeated and subjected to Him Who has been given the Name which is above every other name.

Chapter 4: ANGELIC FELLOW-SERVANTS

The angels of God possess varying degrees of authority and power. They are beings with intelligent minds, voices, hands, feet, and complete bodies. They are designed with the ability to transcend all three heavens, (our atmosphere, outer space, and God's Paradise). They also enjoy endless lives. Once they are created, they live eternally, without ever experiencing death. Our present angels also served God's people of all ages before us.

Revelation 19:10 And I fell at his feet to worship him. And he said unto me, See thou do it not: *I am thy fellow servant, and of thy brethren* **that have the testimony of Jesus: worship God: for the testimony of Jesus is the spirit of prophecy.**

Here, an angel is telling the Apostle John not to worship him; he is a servant (a ministering spirit) of John, and of his Christian brethren, (those that have the testimony of Jesus, and those who will after him).

Revelation 22:8-9 And I John saw these things, and heard them. And when I had heard and seen, I fell down to worship before the feet of the angel which shewed me these things. Then saith he unto me, See thou do it not: for *I am thy fellow servant, and of thy brethren the prophets* **and of them which keep the sayings of this Book: worship God.**

Here, John's angel tells him that he is (now) his servant, and that he was the servant of his brethren the prophets which lived before John's time. The angel also declares that he is the servant of them (before or after John) which serve God by keeping the sayings of this Book. Angels have a continuous ministry from generation to generation.

God has created angels to serve every generation of man, but we have the natural tendency to worship higher beings when they visit us. Even John the Revelator, at least twice, yielded to this tendency. I think this may be one reason why, for the most part, angelic ministries remain low key, invisible and unnoticeable. They are sent forth to serve us, to represent God, and to bring glory, honor and praise unto Him.

Psalms 148:1-6 Praise ye the Lord. Praise ye the Lord from the heavens: praise Him in the heights. Praise ye Him, all His angels: praise ye Him, all His hosts. Praise ye Him, sun and moon: praise Him, all ye stars of light. Praise Him, ye heavens of heavens, and ye waters that be above the heavens. Let them praise the Name of the Lord: for He commanded, and they were created. He hath also stablished them for ever and ever: He hath made a decree which shall not pass.

Along with the sun, moon, stars and heavens, angels were created and established for ever and ever. God decreed from the beginning of His creation that they should exist eternally, and that decree shall not be made void, shall not pass away.

Chapter 5: ANGELS UNAWARES

Although the saints who lived before us have gone on to Heaven to be with the Lord, their angels have remained with us to minister for us. These fellow-servants of our brethren can minister in the same anointings for us as they did for those before us.

As the angels had special charges over God's servants in the past and delivered them from evils, they continue to do so in their ministry for God's people today.

Psalms 34:7 The angel of the Lord encampeth round about them that fear Him, and delivereth them.

Psalms 91:11-12 For He shall give His angels charge over thee, to keep thee in all thy ways. They shall bear thee up in their hands, lest thou dash thy foot against a stone.

As the angels gave voice to God's servants in the past, they can give us utterance also; they work in concert with the Holy Ghost which is in us.

Malachi 2:7 For the Priest's lips should keep knowledge, and they should seek the Law at his mouth: for he is the messenger of the Lord of hosts.

The Hebrew word *malak,* translated "messenger" here, is most often translated "angel." The angels speak God's words. Some messages which identify God as the speaker came, in fact, by angels, as we have already observed in the context of Moses and his "burning bush" experience. Similarly, some messages which identify human preachers as the speakers may in fact have come by angels giving words to God's servants. The human servant is not the angel, but is related to him insofar as he is voicing his words.

God sent John the Baptist, a human preacher, to prepare the way of the Lord, (Matthew 3:1-3). However, the Prophet Malachi, referring to John the Baptist, wrote that God sent His "angel" (Hebrew: *malak,* "messenger") to prepare the way for Him. John, a man of God, was called an "angel."

Malachi 3:1a I will send My messenger, and he shall prepare the way before Me.

On another occasion, an angelic messenger was thought to be a "man" (Hebrew: *iysh,* "of humankind") of God:

Judges 13:6 Then the woman came and told her husband, saying, *A man of God* came unto me, and his countenance was like the countenance of an angel of God, very terrible: but I asked him not whence he was, neither told he me his name.

Oftentimes it is difficult to tell whether a messenger of God is in fact a man, or an angel. (By no coincidence, the word "evangelist," which means "messenger of good news," contains the word "angel.") Hence our commandment to show brotherly love and hospitality to the *stranger*—he might be an angel with a message.

Hebrews 13:1-2 Let brotherly love continue. Be not forgetful to entertain strangers: for thereby some have entertained angels unawares.

Hebrews 13:1-2 (niv) Keep on loving each other as brothers. Do not forget to entertain strangers, for by so doing *some people have entertained angels without knowing it.*

The angels ministered in warfare in the past, as the visions of the Prophet Daniel plainly show us (Daniel 10:13), and they are still involved in wars today—spiritual ones, and natural ones. And as they often went unseen in biblical battles (we often entertain angels *without knowing it, unawares),* they often go unnoticed in our battles also.

2Samuel 5:22-25 (tev) Then the Philistines went back to Rephaim Valley and occupied it again. Once more David consulted the Lord, Who answered, "Don't attack them from here, but go around and get ready to attack them from the other side, near the balsam trees. When you hear the sound of marching in the treetops, then attack because I will be marching ahead of you to defeat the Philistine army." David did what the Lord had commanded, and was able to drive the Philistines back from Geber all the way to Gezer.

"When you hear a marching in the treetops..." Who do you suppose did the marching? The Lord had said, "I will be marching ahead of you," but He no doubt employed angelic troops as well, even though there is no specific mention of them here. As we follow the Lord, He goes before us and fights our battles. Yet He also gives His angels charge over us to guard and guide us in all our ways. And, although we do not always notice the activities of the angels (God doesn't show us everything), the events surrounding our victories are, more often than not, caused by them.

Some angels are especially empowered to bring judgments.

a) earthquakes:

Matthew 28:2 And, behold, there was a great earthquake: for the angel of the Lord descended from Heaven, and came and rolled back the stone from the door, and sat upon it.

b) storms:

Revelation 7:1 And after these things I saw four angels standing on the four corners of the earth, holding the four winds of the earth, that the

wind should not blow on the earth, nor on the sea, nor on any tree.

c) pestilence:

1Chronicles 21:14-15 So the Lord sent pestilence upon Israel: and there fell of Israel seventy thousand men. And God sent an angel unto Jerusalem to destroy it: and as he was destroying it, the Lord beheld, and He repented Him of the evil, and said to the angel that destroyed, It is enough, stay now thine hand. And the angel of the Lord stood by the threshingfloor of Ornan the Jebusite.

d) a physical condition:

Luke 1:18-20 And Zacharias said unto the angel, Whereby shall I know this? for I am an old man, and my wife well stricken in years. And the angel answering said unto him, I am Gabriel, that stand in the presence of God; and am sent to speak unto thee, and to shew thee these glad tidings. And, behold, thou shalt be dumb, and not able to speak, until the day that these things shall be performed, because thou believest not my words, which shall be fulfilled in their season.

e) persecution:

Psalms 35:5-6 Let the angel of the Lord chase them. Let their way be dark and slippery: and let the angel of the Lord persecute them.

f) death:

Acts 12:21-23 Upon a set day Herod, arrayed in royal apparel, sat upon

his throne, and made an oration unto them. And the people gave a shout, saying, It is the voice of a god, and not of a man. And immediately the angel of the Lord smote him, because he gave not God the glory: and he was eaten of worms, and gave up the ghost.

There is also an innumerable amount of other kinds of judgments which can come from God, and they are executed by the ministries of angels. They don't play. There is an innumerable company of angels (Hebrews 12:22), and they own an innumerable amount of abilities.

Some angels are especially anointed to bring blessings.

a) miracles:

1Kings 19:5-8 And as he lay and slept under a juniper tree, behold, then an angel touched him, and said unto him, Arise and eat. And he looked, and, behold, there was a cake baken on the coals, and a cruse of water at his head. And he did eat and drink, and laid him down again. And the angel of the Lord came again the second time, and touched him, and said, Arise and eat; because the journey is too great for thee. And he arose, and did eat and drink, and went in the strength of that meat forty days and forty nights unto Horeb the mount of God.

b) rescue, deliverance, and help:

Acts 5:19 The angel of the Lord by night opened the prison doors, brought them forth and said, Go, stand and speak in the temple to the people all the words of this life.

c) prophecies:

Revelation 1:1 The revelation of Jesus Christ, which God gave unto Him, to shew unto His servants things which must shortly come to pass; and He sent and signified it by His angel unto His servant John.

d) direction, leadings, and guidance:

Acts 10:22 And they said, Cornelius the centurion, a just man, and one that feareth God, and of good report among all the nation of the Jews, was warned from God by an holy angel to send for thee into his house, and to hear words of thee.

e) encouragement:

Acts 27:23-25 And now I exhort you to be of good cheer: for there shall be no loss of any man's life among you, but of the ship. For there stood by me this night the angel of God, whose I am, and whom I serve, Saying, Fear not, Paul; thou must be brought before Caesar: and, lo, God hath given thee all them that sail with thee. Wherefore, sirs, be of good cheer: for I believe God, that it shall be even as it was told me.

f) protection:

Psalms 91:11-12 For He shall give His angels charge over thee, to keep thee in all thy ways. They shall bear thee up in their hands, lest thou dash thy foot against a stone.

Psalms 34:7 The angel of the Lord encampeth round about them that

fear Him, and delivereth them.

An unlimited amount of other kinds of blessings that we may need from God also comes by the ministries of the angels. They minister for us with power from above because the things of earth (and often the people of earth) can't help us.

Some angels can both bless and judge. The angel Gabriel made Zacharias unable to speak for several months (Luke 1:20), and he also favored and prophesied to the Virgin Mary, (Luke 1:26-38).

Chapter 6: ANGELIC PROVIDENCE

Some angels do not minister in supernatural demonstrations as much as others. Even though they are all supernatural beings with powers and abilities far beyond those of mortal men, they usually keep a very low profile. This way we will keep our eyes on the Captain of the Lord's hosts (Jesus), and not on the hosts (angels). It also keeps our faith working when we do not see what they are doing.

Genesis 24:7 The Lord God of Heaven, which took me from my father's house, and from the land of my kindred, and which spake unto me, saying, Unto thy seed will I give this land; He shall send His angel before thee, and thou shalt take a wife unto my son from thence.

In sending his servant out to find a wife for his son Isaac, Abraham realized that the angel of the Lord will go before and prosper him. Well, the angel did go out before and prosper him, as his servant later acknowledges (Genesis

24:40), but there was no visible evidence of the angel's presence: he made no supernatural demonstration whatsoever. If he had, then the servant would not have presented a "fleece" before the Lord (verse 14), and would not have doubted whether the Lord had made his journey prosperous when the fleece was answered, (verse 21).

Further, when this servant realized that the Lord had indeed prospered his journey, and praised Him for it, he said that the Lord had led him, (Genesis 24:27). In the Bible, when angels manifested themselves supernaturally, they were usually acknowledged in some way. But not here. The angel of the Lord is acknowledged beforehand and afterward, but ministered invisibly—behind the fleece and providences—throughout the journey. In all the particulars, he remained completely unnoticed. Biblical events involved angels even when they were not recognized.

In circumstances in our lives today, whether or not we see supernatural manifestations of angels, we can be sure that they are ministering for us, working in our prayers, defeating our enemies, prospering our paths, and bringing to pass the will of the Lord. And, although we should not be quick to present fleeces before the Lord—we are to walk by faith, and not by sights and signs, (2Corinthians 5:7)—He often gives us little hints here and there of what He's doing. Gideon sensed that the Lord could become angry because of his "fleece," so he spoke in a tone of holy fear when requesting of the Lord a supernatural sign.

Judges 6:39-40 And Gideon said unto God, Let not thine anger be hot against me, and I will speak but this once: let me prove, I pray Thee, but this once with the fleece; let it now be dry only upon the fleece, and upon all the ground let there be dew. And God did so that night: for it was dry upon the fleece only, and there was dew on all the ground.

When asking God to confirm by a supernatural sign a leading of His Spirit which we ought to be believing and obeying by faith, we might grieve Him. God could have become angry at Gideon if he would have continued requiring a sign from God, as Gideon was sensitive enough to perceive, so He might become angry at such requests from us, too. However, when we obey even the simplest of the leadings of God, we can discern all kinds of activity which confirms God's involvement, and sense clear evidences of angelic ministry as well.

Psalms 34:7 The angel of the Lord encampeth round about them that fear Him, and delivereth them.

The angel of God "encampeth" ("abides, dwells and rests") with those who serve the Lord, and gives them favor. When we put all the circumstances of our lives in the Lord's hands and trust Him to take care of the matters concerning us, we can be sure He will send his angels to be with us and give us favor. A new job, perhaps one which we did not qualify for, can be granted us when God, by His angel, gives us favor with an employer. A difficult relationship can become pleasant with such favor, too. God's favor can open any door and no man can close it!

Psalms 91:11-12 For He shall give His angels charge over thee, to keep thee in all thy ways. They shall bear thee up in their hands, lest thou dash thy foot against a stone.

When God gives His angels charge over us, it's not always in supernatural ways or in dangerous situations, as Psalms 91 specifically speaks of. The angels' charge over us will keep us in all our ways. They bear us up in their hands so that we will not dash our foot against any stone—that is to say, so that we will not be hindered in any way in any area of our lives. Remember, salvation involves deliverance in every area of our lives—not only rescue from temporal dangers, but also assistance in temporal matters. As we saw in Chapter 5, we often entertain angels unawares in the normal situations and circumstances of daily life.

Chapter 7: EVIL ANGELS

Not only are there good angels that minister for us, but there are also wicked angels which war against us.

Ephesians 6:12 For we wrestle not against flesh and blood, but against principalities, against powers, against the rulers of the darkness of this world, against spiritual wickedness in high places.

Ephesians 6:12 (niv) For our struggle is not against flesh and blood, but against the rulers, against the authorities, against the powers of this dark world and against the spiritual forces of evil in the heavenly realms.

A lot of things which are characteristic of and attributable to the angelic ranks of God are similarly characteristic of and attributable to the angelic ranks of the devil and his cohorts. They were created by God, are organized, have names and titles, have varied ranks, responsibilities and powers, are preoccupied with matters concerning men, and they knew our ancestors before us, (as did our angelic fellow-servants).

In addition, evil angels can also manifest themselves in the following ways:

a) operate in spectacular miracles, signs, and wonders:

2Thessalonians 2:9 (amp) The coming [of the lawless one, the Antichrist] is through the activity and working of Satan, and will be attended by great power and with all sorts of [pretended] miracles and signs and delusive marvels—[all of them] lying wonders.

b) operate covertly and unnoticed with tricky strategies:

Ephesians 6:11 Put on the whole armour of God, that ye may be able to stand against the *wiles of the devil.*

2Corinthians 2:11 (amp) To keep Satan from getting the advantage over us: for we are not ignorant of his *wiles and intentions.*

c) can inspire and partake in visions, trances, out-of-body experiences, and supernatural voices:

Matthew 24:24 For there shall arise false Christs, and false prophets, and shall shew great signs and wonders; insomuch that, if it were possible, they shall deceive the very elect.

d) can give voice to human mouths:

1Kings 22:19-22 And he said, Hear thou therefore the Word of the Lord: I saw the Lord sitting on His throne, and all the host of Heaven standing by Him on His right hand and on His left. And the Lord said, Who shall persuade Ahab, that he may go up and fall at Ramoth-gilead? And one said on this manner, and another said on that manner. And there came

forth a spirit, and stood before the Lord, and said, I will persuade him. And the Lord said unto him, Wherewith? And he said I will go forth, and I will be a lying spirit in the mouth of all his prophets. And He said, Thou shalt persuade him, and prevail also: go forth, and do so.

e) can order natural events:

1Thessalonians 2:18 (amp) Because it was our will to come to you. [I mean that] I Paul, again and again [wanted to come], but *Satan hindered and impeded us.*

1Thessalonians 2:18 (tlb) We wanted very much to come and I, Paul, tried again and again, but Satan *stopped* us.

f) can transact business between the earth and heavens:

Job 1:6 Now there was a day when the sons of God came to present themselves before the Lord, and Satan came also among them.

g) can be manifested as a storm:

Luke 8:23-24 But as they sailed He fell asleep: and there came down a storm of wind on the lake; and they were filled with water, and were in jeopardy. And they came to Him, and awoke Him, saying, Master, Master, we perish. Then He arose, and rebuked the wind and the raging of the water: and they ceased, and there was a calm.

h) can be manifested as lightning:

Luke 10:18 And He said unto them, I beheld Satan as lightning fall from Heaven.

i) can take on the form of a man:

2Corinthians 11:14-15 And no marvel; for Satan himself is transformed into an angel of light. Therefore it is no great thing if his ministers also be transformed as the ministers of righteousness; whose end shall be according to their works.

j) can take on the form of an animal:

Revelation 20:2 And he laid hold on the dragon, that old serpent, which is the Devil, and Satan, and bound him a thousand years.

There are also many other forms which evil angels can take on. As a matter of fact, their forms and ministries can seem so similar to God's angels that they can, at times, appear as them and deceive people:

Galatians 1:8 But though we, or an angel from Heaven, preach any other gospel unto you than that which we have preached unto you, let him be accursed.

That Paul would warn against anyone who would preach a false gospel, even an angel from Heaven, shows us that the devil can send us one of his evil angels with the appearance of a good angel and with a message purportedly from God. Evil angels originally were angels of God until they fell from grace, therefore they know some things about them and are partly able to imitate and appear as them.

Revelation 12:7-9 And there was war in Heaven: Michael and his angels fought against the dragon; and the dragon fought and his angels, And prevailed not; neither was their place found any more in Heaven. And the great dragon was cast out, that old serpent, called the Devil, and Satan, which deceiveth the whole world: he was cast out into the earth, and his angels were cast out with him.

As with good angels, we should not be ignorant concerning the ways and ministries of the devil and his evil angels. Receiving assistance from the former largely depends on us, and so does overcoming the strategies of the latter. A biblical and practical understanding of angelic principalities and powers (both good and evil ones) is invaluable to victory in spiritual warfare.

One of the most important truths which we, as Christians, must know, is that Jesus Christ has given us all the power we can ever need in order to overcome evil forces.

Luke 10:19 (tev) Listen! I have given you authority, so that you can walk on snakes and scorpions and overcome all the power of the enemy, and nothing will hurt you.

Chapter 8: SERVING GOD RELEASES ANGELS

To benefit most from the ministries of God's angels, we must, first of all, be Christians. Sinners, who are outside the Household of God, are outside of His protection, and within Satan's jurisdiction.

Ephesians 2:1-2 (amp) And you [He made alive], when you were dead

[slain] by [your] trespasses and sins. In which at one time you walked habitually. You were following the course and fashion of this world—were under the sway of the tendency of this present age—following the prince of the power of the air. (You were *obedient to him and were under his control,*) the [demon] spirit that still constantly works in the sons of disobedience—the careless, the rebellious and the unbelieving, who go against the purposes of God.

2Corinthians 4:3 (tev) For if the Gospel we preach is hidden, it is hidden only from those who are being lost.

The ministering spirits of God can help anyone receive assistance on occasion, as we read earlier. Sinners can also receive help from God's angels, so that they may have another opportunity to be saved. However, they are more often without that help because they live contrary to the ways of God and angels. Inasmuch as they go against the purposes of God in their beliefs, lifestyle, behavior and disposition, they are being lost and not receiving deliverance from evils or rescue from dangers. The angels are primarily sent forth to guard and protect Christians—those who love and honor the Lord Jesus Christ and bring glory to Him in their beliefs, lifestyle, behavior and disposition.

Psalms 34:7 (tev) His angels guard those who honor the Lord and rescues *them* from danger.

Psalms 145:20 (tev) He protects *everyone who loves Him,* but He will destroy the wicked.

Becoming a Christian transfers us out of the kingdom of darkness and into the Kingdom of God's dear Son, Jesus Christ:

Colossians 1:13 Who hath delivered us from the power of darkness, and hath translated us into the Kingdom of His dear Son.

It is within the domain of the Kingdom of Jesus that the angels are most able to minister for us unhindered—not occasionally, but always and in all ways. But simply becoming a part of God's Kingdom by accepting Jesus as our personal Savior is only the beginning. We must also walk in agreement with Jesus (by obeying the will of God) if we want the angels to be with us, because they walk in agreement with Him. There are degrees of relationship with God and degrees of walking in His will, (Romans 12:2). More often and in more ways than we may realize, angels are either released or hindered by our conversation and lifestyle.

Psalms 35:27b Let the Lord be magnified, which hath pleasure in the prosperity of His servant.

Psalms 103:21 Bless ye the Lord, all ye His hosts; ye ministers of His, that do His pleasure.

The ministering spirits, angelic hosts of God, do His pleasure, what pleases Him. The prosperity and success of His servants pleases Him. If we serve Him, we will prosper by their ministry and enjoy godly success.

Chapter 9: TONGUES OF ANGELS

1Corinthians 13:1a   Though I speak with the tongues of men and of angels.

Psalms 103:20 Bless the Lord, ye His angels, that excel in strength, that do His commandments, hearkening unto the voice of His Word.

The angels of God excel when it comes to strength; they own strength of an excellent order, from Above. They do His commandments, His pleasure, and do not rebel against Him as Lucifer did, (Isaiah 14:12). They also hearken unto the voice of His Word.

Matthew 14:31a And He shall send His angels with a great sound of a trumpet.

The voice of God is as a great sound of a trumpet (as many other Scriptures also affirm), and is instrumental to dispatch angels. The voice of His servants is also symbolized in Scripture as a trumpet, and can also instruct, direct and dispatch angels.

Isaiah 58:1 Cry aloud, spare not, lift up thy voice like a trumpet, and shew My people their transgression, and the house of Jacob their sins.

A man of God prophesied to the Priest Eli of the things that the Lord will do in Israel, (1Samuel 2:27-36). He will cut off Eli and his household for their unfaithfulness to the Lord, and will raise up in his stead a faithful Priest. Immediately after that prophecy was spoken, the Lord called the young Prophet Samuel by an audible voice, confirmed the prophecy, and began to bring it to pass, (1Samuel 3:1-14). It was fulfilled about a century later through the Priest Zadok (2Samuel 8:17), and ultimately through Christ, our Great and Faithful High Priest, (Hebrews 3:1-2).

From that prophecy to the coming of Christ, angels ministered throughout, diligently hearkening unto the prophetic voice of God's Word.

The Christian disciple Ananias had prophesied to Saul of Tarsus (the Apostle Paul) that he would see the Lord and hear the voice of His mouth, (Acts 22:12-15). Soon afterward, Paul did indeed receive such a visitation of the Lord, (Galatians 1:11-12). And throughout his ministry, he continued to receive an abundance of supernatural visions and revelations of the Lord, (cf. 2Corinthians 12:1-4).

Although they may not be specifically mentioned in these instances, the angels played a significant role in delivering God's audible message to Samuel, and revelations of Jesus to Paul. The prophetic words of God's servants sounded as a trumpet and dispatched angels to bring them to pass. Beyond a doubt, this is one reason why God encourages us to prophesy by His Spirit.

1Corinthians 14:1 Follow after charity, and desire spiritual gifts, but rather that ye may prophesy.

1Corinthians 14:5 I would that ye all spake with tongues, but rather that ye prophesied: for greater is he that prophesieth than he that speaketh with tongues, except he interpret, that the church may receive edifying.

1Corinthians 14:31 For ye may all prophesy one by one, that all may learn, and all may be comforted.

1Corinthians 14:39 Wherefore, brethren, covet to prophesy, and forbid

not to speak with tongues.

Numbers 11:29 And Moses said unto him, Enviest thou for my sake? Would God that all the Lord's people were prophets, and that the Lord would put His Spirit upon them!

In all kinds of prayers and prophecies, our anointed voices play a key role because they speak distinct words, and effect distinct responses from the angels. I can put angels to work for me by speaking with other tongues by faith.

1Corinthians 13:1a (tev) I may be able to speak the languages ...even of angels.

The Apostle Paul makes mention here of "languages," of "angels" (both words plural). The King James Version has it, "tongues of angels." This could generally mean words of kindness, good advice, or encouragement, because angelic words often are as such—but much more is intended. Paul prayed a lot with other tongues (1Corinthians 14:18), and was delivered out of all kinds of persecutions, afflictions and perils, (2Corinthians 11:23-33; 2Timothy 3:10-11). No doubt the angels helped Paul as they hearkened unto the words of God which he voiced in their languages, *in other tongues.*

The angels are able to communicate in the languages of earth and of Heaven. Although we don't always know which words to use in prayer, the Holy Spirit helps us by giving us *utterances in the spirit,* (Romans 8:26). Those utterances, which Paul also refers to as *mysteries (secrets) in the spirit* (1Corinthians 14:2), may involve the dispatching of angels to minister for us. This occurs much more than we can ever realize. When we pray with other tongues in our worship to the Lord, or in intercession, or in spiritual warfare, or in prayers of contrition, petition or supplication, we don't always perceive them but angels are sent forth to minister unto us in response.

Just as the angels walk in concert with Jesus, they also talk in concert with Him. We, too, should not only walk, but also talk in concert with Jesus if we want the angels to minister in response to the voice of our words.

1Corinthians 14:15 What is it then? I will pray with the spirit, and I will pray with the understanding also: I will sing with the spirit, and I will sing with the understanding also.

Praying with the spirit (in other tongues) and praying with the understanding (in our regular language) are both instrumental and necessary in receiving help from angels. When we walk with God in a general way, they minister for us in general ways. But when we walk in His perfect will, then they can minister for us in more specific, perfect and excellent ways. Well, it's the same thing with our prayers. When we pray generalized prayers, the angels minister in response in generalized ways. But when we talk with God in specific Holy Spirit-blessed prayers, in His own language (other tongues), then the angels will minister for us in more specific, perfect and excellent ways. They are sent forth to serve us, to hearken unto (hear and obey) the voice of God's words which we speak, whether or not we understand those words.

The angels are equipped to assist us in any and all things concerning the Christian life. They are not limited by time and space and, even when we don't perceive them, they are always near and ready to serve us. As we have already observed, they partake in much more of the activities of our lives than we give them credit for—both in supernatural things, and in natural things.

By being reconciled unto God in the new birth, by living in line with His will, and by believing in the supernatural realm which His Word enlightens us to, we can inherit salvation in all its merits. By serving God with all our hearts and lives, we can receive assistance in all its forms by the supernatural ministries of the angels.

Chapter 10: QUESTIONS & ANSWERS

Galatians 1:6-12 I marvel that ye are so soon removed from Him that called you into the grace of Christ unto another gospel: Which is not another; but there be some that trouble you, and would pervert the gospel of Christ. But though we, or an angel from Heaven, preach any other gospel unto you than that which we have preached unto you, let him be accursed. As we said before, so say I now again, If any man preach any other gospel unto you than that ye have received, let him be accursed. For do I now persuade men, or God? or do I seek to please men? for if I yet pleased men, I should not be the servant of Christ. But I certify you, brethren, that the gospel which was preached of me is not after man. For I neither received it of man, neither was I taught it, but by the revelation of Jesus Christ.

Acts 16:30-31 Sirs, what must I do to be saved? And they said, Believe on the Lord Jesus Christ, and thou shalt be saved, and thy house.

Salvation, reconciliation to God, forgiveness of sins, and being born-again, comes by believing in and accepting Jesus Christ as one's own personal Lord and Savior. Understanding the message of the Gospel, too, comes by the revealing of Jesus Christ to one's soul. Many religions have been founded on false revelations, often delivered by fallen angels, which don't give glory to Jesus. They neither begin nor end with Him, though He may play a role in them, or simply be mentioned in their literature. But the Bible teaches us that Jesus Christ is to be the beginning and the end of our relationship with God and our religion, and that He is to be acknowledged and glorified always and in all ways throughout.

For not having focused on Jesus, many people, even whole nations and cultures, have gone into error. Everyone seems to have an opinion about God, religious matters, spiritual things, and angels. There are so many contradicting philosophies. There is so much confusion and discord, not surprisingly, simply because of a lack of understanding, believing or following what the Bible says.

We ought to give earnest heed to God's own doctrine about Himself and spiritual things, including angels. That we are Christians, truly born-again and Spirit-filled, does not make us exempt from erroneous teaching along these lines. As we read above, Paul, in sternly warning against receiving revelations from false preachers and false angels, was writing to Pentecostals—people who believe in Jesus and ought to know the Word of God. Even today, when so much excellent teaching about angels has been given the Body of Christ, there still seems to be a lack of knowledge in this area.

I was shocked some years ago when a young lady, who had been in Church all of her life, didn't understand the divinity of Jesus. "Isn't He like an angel?" This was her way of trying to teach me about Jesus, for she was one of my first Bible teachers. Well, I realized then that many Christians don't study the Bible, and for not understanding the ministry of angels according to the Bible, many neglect the great salvation (deliverance, rescue, assistance, help) that is available to us by them. When we understand who we are in Christ, who the angels are, and how they operate, we can enjoy the great salvation brought about by them. (As I showed in Chapter 2, this "salvation" is distinguished from the redemption that is in Christ through repentance. A person can be born-again and yet not enjoy the benefits of the salvation that is rightfully theirs in Christ.)

I think I have covered the most important aspects of the angels in this book—many doctrinal, and many practical. I have shown many Scripture verses to which the reader ought to refer to verify that my statements are so. Although I have had many supernatural visions involving angels, and have heard them speak to me on many occasions, I have not shared these experiences here because that is not the purpose of this book. (I share many of my supernatural experiences in my other books.) Here, I simply want to establish a concise, comprehensive presentation of the ministry of angels as the Bible teaches about it, and, if God would permit, allow you to enjoy your own experiences with them.

If there are still some questions, after referring to the verses I have listed and searching the Scriptures some more, perhaps the following will bring more understanding. Where the Bible is silent or unclear, I attempt to answer with an educated opinion, and indicate so.

30 Questions & Answers About Angels

1. What are angels? Angels are beings which God created to serve Him. They were not created in the image of God as human beings are, for the Bible says it only of man that God created him in His own image, (Genesis 1:26-27). Angels were created in eternity past before anything else was ever created, for they were employed in the creation and construction of the entirety of the universe.

Angels represent attributes and characteristics of God. Each angel has a uniqueness about him through which a particular character trait of God can be shown. Even among a group of a million angels of similar rank and anointing, there can be found individuality because God created each of them to worship Him of their own volition and have personal relationship with Him.

2. Who is the angel of the Lord? He is the Lord's messenger, the messenger of the Lord. At times, he may be an angel sent by the Lord Jesus; at times, He is Jesus Himself, as a Messenger sent by the Father. The way the Bible reports the operations of angels and of the "angel of the Lord" is not absolutely clear and comprehensive, so both of these interpretations can be fitting. Jesus is called the Messenger (Hebrew: *malak,* "angel") of the Covenant (Malachi 3:1), and angels are called messengers, (Psalms 104:4).

3. Are angels everywhere (omnipresent)? No, not in the sense of being absolutely in every spot that exists in all creation. They move around and travel, they visit people and places, and they are absent from certain places. They can go anywhere that God sends them in Heaven or in earth, but, whether as a myriad of angels or an individual angel, they are limited to a certain location at a time. Even Jesus, as He now is in His glorified physical body, is limited to being at only one place at a time. Only God is everywhere, and that is by the Holy Spirit.

4. Are angels all-knowing (omniscient)? No, only God is all knowing. Even Jesus Himself doesn't know the time of His return, (Mark 13:32). But the angels are very much in the know concerning a whole lot more than us. When they visit us they may seem to be all-knowing as far as concerns our lives and situations because they see much more than we do, know details about our past, present, and future which we do not know or understand, and they have God's wisdom for our lives in areas that we often don't.

5. Are angels all-powerful (omnipotent)? Only God is all-powerful and almighty. The angels, however, are extremely strong and can do things which the strongest men on earth cannot do, (Matthew 28:2). Some angels are stronger than others (Daniel 10:13). If we see some sort of a vision of an angel we might be able to tell whether he is of a high position in the hosts of Heaven, and what is his area of expertise, by his size and by his garments. But that is no comparison to the omnipotence of Almighty God, at Whose very presence and countenance the heavens and the earth shall flee away on the Great White Throne Judgment Day, (Revelation 20:11). The Word of God says only of Him:

Luke 1:37 For with God nothing shall be impossible.

6. Are men greater than angels? or lower than angels? In some ways angels are greater than men, and in other ways men are greater. Angels have more supernatural ability than we do: they're stronger, never get tired, weak or sick, they don't need to eat or rest, they can fly or be instantly transported from place to place, they can see, hear and know things which we can't, they are able to orchestrate circumstances which are beyond our realm of control, and they can do so much more than these things.

Human beings, on the other hand, although we may be limited in a lot of these things in comparison to the angels, we are greater than they are in some ways. As distinct from all the angels, we are created in the image of God and are made to have dominion and reign over the works of His hands.

By faith in the Lord Jesus as our Savior, we are able to become sons of God, heirs of God and joint-heirs with Jesus Christ. We are seated in Heavenly places in Him, are made to be kings and priests unto Him, and reign with Him. In Heaven, we shall have crowns and sit on thrones and judge angels.

When the Psalmist David asked God, "What is man?" he, by a revelation of the Holy Ghost in the realm of the spirit, saw that man was made to be *just a little lower* than the "Godhead, the Supreme God, Almighty, Judge of all." God made man inferior to no other being but Himself. This is never said of the angels. The *King James Version* has it: "For Thou has made him a little lower than the *angels,"* but most other versions of the Bible correctly translate the original Hebrew word *Elohym* as "God."

Psalms 8:5a (tev) Yet You made him inferior *only to Yourself.*

 The *Revised Standard Version* says, "Yet Thou hast made him *little less than God."* And *Young's Literal Translation* has it, "...And causest him to *lack a little of Godhead."*

7. Is the Devil an angel? Yes, he is a fallen angel, which means that he "fell" from grace and favor with God when he sinned. All angels have a free will, and have the ability to choose whether or not they will obey God. Lucifer (which, after rebelling against God, became the Devil, and Satan) and many of the angels over which he had authority and influence, *chose* to sin and disobey God by an act of their own volition. They freely willed and deliberately intended to disobey God.

Isaiah 14:12-15 How art thou fallen from Heaven, O Lucifer, son of the morning! how art thou cut down to the ground, which didst weaken the nations! For thou hast said in thine heart, I will ascend into Heaven, I will exalt my throne above the stars of God: I will sit also upon the Mount of the congregation, in the sides of the north: I will ascend above the heights of the clouds; I will be like the Most High. Yet thou shalt be brought down to hell, to the sides of the pit.

 God knew from the beginning of His creation that Lucifer would fall and lead a rebellion in Heaven against Him, but He already had a plan—the mystery of the Gospel, which from the beginning has been hidden in God (Colossians 1:26-27)—to redeem man and creation from the lost condition into which

Satan would bring it. God did not cause the rebellion. He is omnipotent, and can order and influence the hearts of kings (Proverbs 21:1), but He does not control anyone's will by enforcing His will superiorly to their's, and He does not author sin. God says of Lucifer that sin was "found" in him:

Ezekiel 28:15 Thou wast perfect in thy ways from the day that thou wast created, till iniquity was found in thee.

There is no salvation for the devil or for any of the fallen angels. They have no mediator before God, so they cannot be forgiven of their sins and restored to fellowship with God. Without the shedding of sacrificial blood, there is no remission of sin, (Hebrews 9:22). And the only blood which is holy and acceptable before God, and able to wash away sins, is the precious Blood of Jesus Christ, the sacrificial Lamb of God which takes away the sin of the world, (John 1:29). Jesus, in Whose own image we are created, came to earth in the form of man, to die for and redeem man. The angels have no such redeemer.

From the time of Lucifer's fall until now, His name is "Satan," and he is called "the devil." And, from then until now, his angels (all the fallen angels) are called "devils" or "demons;" people usually refer to them as fallen angels only when they are making the point that they once were [good] angels. (Although these fallen angels are called "demons," there is a school of thought which attributes this term to a different class of fallen spirits, namely, the order of earthly creatures which existed and were destroyed before the time of Adam and Eve; cf. Jeremiah 4:23-28).

8. Are angels still being created? The Bible doesn't say so, but I think so because God is always creating new things—both on earth and throughout the universe—and there is still human procreation; therefore, it makes the most sense that new angels would be made to serve in those new things. There are not evil angels being created. God is the only Creator, and He only creates good things. Evil angels are those which were good and became evil by sinning.

9. Can angels still sin today and fall?   After the fall of Lucifer and the angels that followed him (Isaiah 14:12), there is no biblical account of other angels sinning and falling from favor with God. However, given that angels have a free will (they are not as much like robots as we often think), it may be possible for them to do their own thing and sin. But since they are personally acquainted with heavenly blessings in God's presence, and are familiar with divine things, it is not likely they would want to sin and lose favor with God. And since they can see and know things in the realm of the spirit much more clearly than we can fathom, we may presume that they are able to see Satan and fallen angels and their evil condition and, therefore, have no desire whatsoever to follow in his footsteps.

So the angels, even today, have a free will and the right to choose for themselves whether or not they will serve the Lord.

10. Does everyone have a guardian angel, or many angels? Do some people have more angels than others? What about people who serve the devil? Do they still have a guardian angel until they die?   In my opinion, each and every person that is born on earth is sent a guardian angel who will always be with him until he dies. That angel can have any number of ministering angels under his command, depending on how much that person serves God and needs them. Even people who serve Satan and do evil have at least their guardian angel with them, though he is not able to help them in their evil behavior or lifestyle.

Also, certain distinguished angels, such as the Archangel Michael, may visit and minister to us, but that doesn't mean that they are our guardian angels. Besides our own personal guardian angels which are always with us, there are special angels which can temporarily come to us and grant a special blessing.

11. Are angels everywhere in the universe, or just in our local galaxy where God's main focus of attention is? Since angels operate in all the three heavens, including outer space (the second heaven), we may conclude that they operate in all the galaxies which are still being created, expanded and constructed throughout the whole universe. Earth, however, is indeed God's main focus of attention because this is where mankind, His greatest creation, lives, and this is where Jesus came and gave His life a ransom for us. The importance and uniqueness of earth, mankind, and all God's doings here—past, present and future—is a good indication of how important and unique is the ministry of angels here.

12. Since the angels are always with us helping us in everything, what is their involvement in our private doings, such as when we bathe, dress, or have sex? Do they see everything, do they become embarrassed, do they turn away at such times? I Believe that they see and assist us in everything, but, being perfectly holy and perfectly wise, they are not embarrassed by our human activities and personal idiosyncrasies. When we do our private things, the angels automatically put their thinking in a certain mode which—though they are still there and aware—seems to place a veil between us and them for privacy's sake. They are able to respect our privacy without leaving us and without embarrassing us, and we never need to instruct them to do so.

When there's inappropriate behavior or sin in our private activities, the angels may attempt to order our doings aright by whispering or placing thoughts in our minds, or by doing something else in their attempt to correct us.

13. Can the angels minister for us automatically if we do not acknowledge or dispatch them specifically? Do we have to be specifically instructed by the Lord and anointed to dispatch angels, and how specific are we supposed to be in our dispatching them? Why do bad things happen to people that serve God? We can be as specific in dispatching angels in our service as is necessary and appropriate, as long as there is sufficient biblical support for our prayer. For example, we may always acknowledge the angels for protection and assistance in general temporal matters, but not in matters in which we are being selfish, carnal or un-Christlike, and certainly not in sin. I always ask and acknowledge their protection when I'm in public, especially when I'm traveling. I also ask them to protect me when I sleep. And whenever I have misplaced something, I ask the angels to help me find it, and they always do.

If we do not acknowledge the angels when we ought to, they are still with us and can still protect us, but there are times when we really need to do so, particularly when God instructs us to. We don't need to be specifically instructed and anointed by God to dispatch angels, but if He so instructs and anoints us, it must be because of a special need at the time. And if we neglect to do so after such a divine leading, it may result in something bad happening. This is why bad things can happen to Christians. In large part, it doesn't matter that we didn't know how to pray about or speak the Word of God to a matter. Jesus said, "For unto whomsoever much is given, of him shall be much required: and to whom men have committed much, of him they will ask the more," (Luke 12:48b). God requires us to learn the things of Him which He has made available to us—and if we don't, it may cost us. "My people are destroyed for a lack of knowledge," (Hosea 4:6).

14. Can the angels preach the Gospel? Why did the angel tell Cornelius to send for Peter? Angels can proclaim God's messages. The Law of God was given (arranged, ordained, appointed, prescribed, commanded) by the instrumentality of angels, (Galatians 3:19). During the Great Tribulation, an angel will fly in the sky and preach the Everlasting Gospel to everyone on earth and direct people to God, (Revelation 14:6). Even today, and all throughout the Church Age, people testify of being directed to Jesus by an angelic leading of some kind. Usually the angel will lead a person to someone who can help him pray to be born-again, but it may also occur right there and then when the angel speaks.

It is by the Holy Spirit that one can be born-again, (John 3:5). God would usually have the Gospel preached by one who has been born-again and who can—because of his own experience—bring conviction of sin to a sinner and lead him in the new birth. Angels cannot relate to sin and cannot be born-again, so they cannot reach the depths of a sinner's heart as can one who's been there. So, the angels can preach, but they can't really reach out to sinners as can those who know exactly where they are and can speak their language from heart to heart. In my opinion, then, it is God's rule to use people to preach His Word of salvation, ("How shall they hear without a *preacher?*" cf. Romans 10:14); however, the angels are always intently involved, as in the matter of Peter and Cornelius, (Acts 10).

15. Are little babies like angels? Do we become angels when we die and go to Heaven? Do angels look like babies? What about cherubim? Angels are of a completely different order of being than humans. A human being is not first born as an angel, can never become as an angel while on earth, and will never become an angel after he dies. As distinguished from angels, human beings are the ones to whom God referred when He said, "Let us make man in Our image, according to Our likeness," (Genesis 1:26). Angels do not look like babies. There is no indication from the Bible that they appear anything but adult, strong, usually masculine, and never with wrinkles, blemishes, missing hair, missing teeth, overly fat or overly skinny. They are always perfect and awesome in sight.

Cherubim (or, cherubs) are among the highest ranking of all God's angels. They guarded the Tree of Life after Adam's fall, and their images were represented on the Ark of the Covenant, on the curtains of the Tabernacle, and on the veil of the Temple. The role of a cherub is to cover, guard and protect God's Shekinah presence from being penetrated. They are ever ready to be dispatched from God's glory to defend His absolute holiness, for they are the most closely related to the Throne, (Psalms 80:1).

In mythology, greeting cards, and religious art, cherubs are depicted as babies. The likeliest explanation for this is that Satan has caused such a depiction of the angels to be perpetuated so as to give the impression that they are—as innocent little babies are—weak, fragile and harmless; that they need not be feared or heeded. Instead, he depicts himself and his cohorts as great, terrible and powerful. But the Bible describes the devil and his demons as powerless against those who serve God (Luke 10:18-20), and God's angels as great, majestic and awesome.

Since angels are "forever young" and have eternity before them, they may indeed have baby-like or childlike characteristics. It may be, therefore, that such a depiction has some justification. A God-inspired vision of angels as babies may represent their agelessness, newness, harmlessness (toward us), innocence, and purity.

16. Is there a divine array among the angelic hosts? Are they organized according to class, rank, and authority? Yes, they have a highly organized heirarchy comprised of many classes of angels, all positioned according to their employments and level of authority. The finite mind cannot fathom the vast extent and excellence of the various angelic orders, but the Bible gives us an undeniable glimpse into them by several specific Scripture references.

Ephesians 1:21 Far above *all principality, and power, and might, and dominion,* and every name that is named, not only in this world, but also in that which is to come.

Here are several classes of angels: principalities, powers, authorities, and there are many more. Cherubim are angels that minister with respect to the Shekinah Glory of God, in Heaven and in earth. Seraphim are angels with a ministry of fire, involved in burning to purify and make holy, (Isaiah 6:1-7).

17. Is there life on other planets or in other galaxies? If so, what is the involvement of angels in them? The angels sang for joy at the creation of planet earth (Job 38:4-7); they knew that ministering for those who shall be heirs of salvation was the purpose for which they were created, (Hebrews 1:14). They were employed in the constructing of the entire universe—all the planets, stars and galaxies—but they were particularly interested in this planet because it was and always will be God's main concern.

As far as there being life on other planets, in my unauthoritative opinion, I think that there is intelligent life out there, entire civilized planets in other galaxies which, for the most part, exist in a sort of fourth, fifth, or other dimension. I think there are dimensions invisible to physical eyesight and technology, where natural physical laws as earthlings understand them cease to apply. And, since Satan and his cohorts were cast down to earth and are limited to our immediate corner of the galaxy, those other civilized, inhabited worlds know only good and not sin and evil. They know that God exists, but don't know Him, are unfamiliar with the life and ministry of Jesus Christ, are not created in God's image, and do not need to be born-again in the same way as humans. They are the "folds" Jesus mentioned that also belong to Him, and which we will be kings and priests over. They also appear and communicate in forms more pleasant, civil, and noble, than fictional stories portray them.

John 10:16 And other sheep I have, which are not of this fold.

Space looks empty because it is beckoning us to come and fill it, spruce it up and do what we want with it once we are glorified with Jesus. Lacking only a little of the Godhead (Psalms 8:5), we are as gods (Psalms 82:6), and we sit in Heavenly places with Christ (Ephesians 2:6), and shall reign with Him, (2Timothy 2:12). In June 2008, Jesus showed me a dream about life on other planets, and said, "I'm looking for people that I can knock some sense into—like you." He is trying to educate us now about what's ahead in eternity.

These views are not unbiblical. Given that the Bible does not give details about extraterrestrial beings other than angels, we are left to conjecture based on the sources of information we do have access to—including scientific and spiritual insights—attempting to scrutinize them with a view from God's Word.

18. Do angels operate the same way in all religions? Or are there certain Christian angels, and certain Buddhist, Muslim, Jewish ones, etc.? Though they always disdain sin and error, the angels tolerate religious and doctrinal shortcomings. They come in God's stead to mediate between Heaven and earth, so they are friendly and considerate, not religious, legalistic, or dogmatic. They may assist people in temporal matters, but are more accessible to and active in ministering for Christians because we are the heirs of God and joint-heirs with Jesus Christ, (Romans 8:17).

The angels ultimately seek to draw all persons unto Jesus because He is the Author of salvation and their Creator. Jesus said, "All power is given unto Me in Heaven and in earth," (Matthew 28:18). "[Jesus] is gone into Heaven, and is on the right hand of God; angels and authorities and powers being made subject unto Him," (1Peter 3:22).

19. Can angels cause something bad to happen, or hurt someone? Yes,

they can and do. Because of their sins, God sent a destroying angel to slay such persons as cruel Nabal (1Samuel 25:38), Herod (Acts 12:23), Ananias and Sapphira (Acts 5:1-10), and such peoples as the Egyptians (Exodus 12:12), the Assyrians (2Chronicles 32:21), and even His own people the Israelites, (1Chronicles 21:15). Often such smiting was not to destroy but to afflict the physical body, as with Elymas the psychic (Acts 13:11), Saul of Tarsus (Acts 9:1-9), and the Patriarch Jacob, (Genesis 32:24-32).

When we sin, we open the door to the devil and he can afflict us in some way. But at times—in unique instances—it is God's own judgment against us being executed by his angels. When this is the case, the affliction will probably be supernatural in nature; it will occur instantly and not normalize by natural means, and may perhaps be of an odd manifestation, as with Herod. When this is the case, repentance of sin and submission to God is the only cure. God said to His own people, "I will go and return to My place, till they acknowledge their offence, and seek My face: in their affliction they will seek Me early," (Hosea 5:15).

20. Can we touch or feel angels? Can they touch or feel us? As real as they are, the angels exist and operate on a spiritual, invisible plane that is unfamiliar and usually inaccessible to us. Seeing and hearing them occurs infrequently, and touching them is rarer still. Even the angels who serve us on earth are incorporeal and, therefore, unlikely to be felt by the human touch— that is, by us trying to touch their "bodies." But it is fairly easy to feel their "presence" when we are in the spirit and minding spiritual things.

Now if an angel chooses to touch our bodies, that, too, can be easy to feel. I have felt such a touch—not just the presence of an angel near me, but the touch of his hand on my body—on many occasions. Though he may touch me more often than I feel his touch, I usually feel it just while I'm having a supernatural vision or dream.

I often feel the release of an angel's hand just at the moment I awaken from a dream from the Lord. This proves to me that it is from the Lord, because His angel's hand or finger is inside my mind during it, producing and directing dream-thoughts according to the message God is giving me at the time.

I think that if we would feel the touch of an angel on a more-or-less regular basis, it would probably be while we are doing the thing we are called of God to do. I'm a prophet anointed in the area of dreams and visions, and that's the area in which I've most often felt the distinct touch of angels. The joy and vibrancy we feel when we are doing what God has called us to do (as we fulfill our God-ordained purpose in life) is doubtless caused, in part, by the life-giving joy and vibrancy of our angels who are close to us. If there is joy in the presence of the angels over a sinner that repents of his sins and begins to walk in the Light (Luke 15:10), then there is also joy in their presence when we daily walk in the Light. Salvation is a daily walk.

This feeling of a touch from an angel is different from a feeling from the Holy Spirit, even though they obviously work together to bless us. When the Holy Spirit is touching us, we will feel Him moving inside us—in our spirit or mind, or manifesting Himself upon our bodies by His [tangible] anointing, usually from the inside out. When it is an angel touching us, we will feel him outside of us as though he is a being with a body separate from ours (because he is).

As an exception to this, we might feel an angel's tangible touch inside our physical body when God is supernaturally healing us by the angel's assistance; he may be playing the role of a doctor performing an operation. Or, an angel can enter our mind and supernaturally plant in us the thoughts of God, as may occur when one is in a *trance* vision.

21. When angels do spiritual warfare, can they fail or be defeated? They are successful at what they do and perfectly efficient in responding to our prayers. But if we fail to summon their assistance, or to do so correctly, the number of angels we need or the role we need them to play can become limited. This is why God always blesses a biblical study on angels, and they seem to "come alive" in our lives then.

No matter how well intentioned people might be, they may have wrong ideas about how to acknowledge the ministries of the angels. The Bible, however, is fairly simple on this subject. Now some people have selfish or unbiblical motives, and the angels cannot accommodate them.

22.   Do angels speak every language on earth? Do they speak unconventionally (slang)? Can they appear as the people they are visiting (Asians, Africans, etc.)? Again, the angels are perfectly efficient at everything they do, so they are able to play any role needed at the time, and communicate in any way necessary, including slang. They are friendly, so they will appear to us in the way they know we will be able to relate to them, and speak accordingly so we will understand them. They may use colloquial expressions, idioms, puns and parables, or speak poetically, sing, or make music, sounds, noises, blasts, or even cause perfect silence. There just seems to be no limit to the methods angels can employ to accomplish their missions.

23. Do angels eat, rest, and change clothes? Do they work shifts? What about angels' (mighty) food? The heavenly manna with which the Israelites were supernaturally fed in the wilderness (Exodus 16:4), was angels' bread— the food of the *mighty ones,* (Psalms 78:23-25). Heaven also has other foods (Revelation 22:1-2), so, as do the saints there, the angels probably eat of them, too. However, neither the saints nor the angels need to eat in Heaven because there is never any hunger or lack of nutrition there. Even on earth, angels don't need to eat, and it is likely they wouldn't enjoy or benefit from our foods. In an extremely rare instance, the Patriarch Abraham prepared food for angels, and they ate (Genesis 18:1-8), no doubt with a divine purpose in mind.

There is always activity in Heaven, and since no one there can ever get tired, there is no need for rest, though there is sitting. The angels, even when they are on earth, also never rest because they are excellent in strength. They may change their garments occasionally, especially when they are being appointed to new tasks. They may also rotate in shifts at their tasks, as we do on earth, as the angel Gabriel seems to indicate, (Daniel 10:12-14).

Although there are always angels with me, some of those who have visited me with messages came only on short assignments—they are *messenger* angels, not *guardian* angels. As such, they are the ones responsible for delivering God's messages to me, but not necessarily for protecting me.

24. What is the role of angels in worship and praise to God? Everything in Heaven is rhythmical and musical: there, the trees and flowers sing, animals sing, and saints and angels sing. So when angels minister to us, even when we don't realize it, it may be with music and song. I'm sure they often whisper tunes in our ears and cause us to start praising God. They are also, together with the Holy Spirit, behind the spontaneous new songs and unpremeditated sounds on our instruments. When we yield to the Holy Spirit, even our playing on instruments can become orchestrated by the angels, whether for a few hours or minutes, or only for a moment or two.

In Church worship and praise the angels beam and get all excited as they participate in our services. Of course, they also dance with those who dance, laugh with those who laugh, and behave drunkenly with those who are drunk with the new wine of the Spirit. When people dance, jump, shake, run or fall, the angels are always right there watching over each one so that our movements are safe and appropriate ones.

25. What is the role of angels in the salvation of souls? They battle against demon forces that are oppressing people, and help to arrange circumstances in their lives in such a way so as to make opportunities for them to hear the Gospel. By influencing their thoughts or their steps; by guiding Christians or Christian literature into their lives; by the working of providences, coincidences, unexpected situations or changes in plans; angels are diligent and constant in all their efforts to direct people to Jesus. And once a person gets born-again, the angels continue to work diligently and constantly to direct him or her. They are ever seeking to bring people more and more into God's perfect will and into His divine purpose which He has designed for their lives.

  The angels are able to work most effectively in guiding souls to Jesus when there are Christians praying for those souls to be saved; especially when the angelic ministry is acknowledged in those prayers. Then, when sinners are converted, there is joy, excitement and shouts of victory among the angels—both in Heaven and on earth.

Luke 15:10 Likewise, I say unto you, there is *joy in the presence of the angels of God* over one sinner that repenteth.

26. Can we "grade" or "judge" our angels on how they are doing? In Heaven, all the redeemed will sit on thrones together with Jesus and bring all things into judgment. We will require all things to be brought into account, even the secretest things now hidden. The books shall be opened—the book of remembrance, the book of works, the book of Life—and eternal destinies and rewards will be determined, even those of the angels who now serve and minister for us. And, since we will be able to pronounce opinion between right and wrong for them, it appears they are teachable and can learn. This gives us all the more reason to represent the Lord and thus make known unto the angels the manifold wisdom of Christ, (Ephesians 3:10).

1Corinthians 6:2-3 (amp)   Do you not know that the saints [the

Christians] will [one day] judge and govern the world? And if the world [itself] is to be judged and ruled by you, are you unworthy and incompetent to try [such petty matters] of the smallest courts of justice? Do you not know also that we [Christians] are to judge the [very] angels and pronounce opinion between right and wrong [for them]? How much more then [as to] matters pertaining to this world and of this life only!

27. Since we will one day judge our angels on how well they have served us, how can we improve their present service to us? How can we acknowledge and cooperate with them, or pray to God about them? We need to have a working knowledge of the ministry of angels according to the Bible. Too many people nowadays have weird notions concerning the angels, and grieve instead of receive from them. A working knowledge of the angels means a general understanding of their nature, purpose, power and accessibility. It means we know that we can call upon them to assist us in the affairs of life—not only in times of crisis, but also in the simplest and most fundamental of daily matters.

I don't call upon the help of angels religiously or ritualistically; I simply make brief and occasional mention of them as I ask God for something. When I'm not in prayer, if I'm going somewhere or doing something, I may go ahead and acknowledge their presence and assistance, but often I do not. Much of their ministry to us is regular and consistent—they're always with us, especially when we are living according to God's will for our lives—so we don't need to tell them to help us in every single thing that we do.

When I do acknowledge the angels and seek their assistance, it's always with a short and simple request: "Angels of God go with me... to the Church... to the store... as I travel on this flight... (or anywhere I may be going)." "Go before me... guide me in this situation... help me find this lost item... help me to do my exercise routine safely... don't let me hurt anyone or get hurt while playing this football game... while boxing or wrestling... while lifting weights... (or whatever the case may be)." "Angels, watch over me as I sleep... protect me as I go here, and there... let me meet the right people... fix circumstances in my favor... open doors for me which God wants open, and let no man or demon close them... close doors for me which God wants closed, and let no man or demon open them."

A working knowledge of the ministry of angels also means that we can boldly come before the throne of God in prayer and ask Him with confidence to send more angels to help us when there's a real need for them:

"Lord God, help me right now by sending more of your angels to come to my aid... to protect me from these evil ones (people or spirits)... to work in this urgent matter..." "Lord, send an angel to stop this blood flow (in an injury)... to assist this medical team (in the hospital)... to get me to my destination quickly and safely (on the street or highway in an emergency)... to remove all these obstacles which are beyond my ability to overcome (whatever the crisis may be), in Jesus' Name."

It seems we can request the assistance of angels in any legitimate and appropriate matter. Besides telling them that we know they are with us, and maybe thanking them, it seems that our communication with them is limited to invoking their help. They are not to be worshiped or revered, as we have already shown, but are created to be dispatched in our service.

Hebrews 1:14 (tlb) No, for the angels are only spirit-messengers sent out to help and care for those who are to receive His salvation.

28. Since angels are not everywhere, how can I tell exactly where they are and where they are not? Is there a way to determine whether there is an angel in a certain location or a certain spot? We don't have to know such specifics, and God would not have us to all the time be minding such details about spiritual things. We should be content to know that, since angels are always with us, they travel alongside us wherever we may go. Our own angels are mobile, just as much so as we are, and can go places where otherwise there aren't any angels. So even if there aren't any angels in a certain place, there will be when we get there.

There is a dynamic working in the realm of the spirit in which an angelic presence is relative to proximity. Angels are more in some places than in others. In Christian homes, churches, and businesses, especially where God is given full right-of-way, there are angels all the time ministering. (Several years ago, a friend working in my bedroom was awestruck by the angelic presence there; he couldn't bear it so he left.) Where there is sin and evil, there will be less angels present. A sinner will have his own guardian angel with him, and others if people are praying for him, but there are not distinguished presences of angels in the places where God is not honored, unless they are evil angels.

Sometimes angels are located in a specific place—a certain property, neighborhood, or a whole city—in a special extraordinary way. In times of revival, the heavens open up and disclose portals in the sky where there are supernatural anointings of the Holy Spirit being manifested, such as occurred in Bethel (the "House of God") when the Lord spoke to His servant Jacob:

Genesis 28:10-13 And he lighted upon *a certain place,* and tarried there all night, because the sun was set; and he took of the stones of that place, and put them for his pillows, and lay down in that place to sleep. And he dreamed, and behold a ladder set up on the earth, and the top of it reached to Heaven: and behold the angels of God ascending and descending *on it.*

When special manifestations of God began in Toronto, Canada, in January,

1994, heavenly angels were commissioned to begin to minister there in a way that they had not been doing before then. On Father's Day, 1995, in Pensacola, Florida, special angels were dispatched from Heaven to begin ministering in that city to accompany the new anointing of the Holy Spirit which God began to release then, beginning with the Brownsville Assembly of God Church. Everywhere there is an *open heaven* through which Heaven visits earth, angels are involved there in a way that they are not involved a city away, a neighborhood away, or even a foot away.

Psalms 18:9-10   He bowed the heavens also, and came down: and darkness was under his feet. And He rode upon a cherub, and did fly: yea, He did fly upon the wings of the wind.

When God "comes down" by riding upon a cherub (an angel), and flies upon the wings of the wind, His [angelic] presence is strictly limited to the corner, border, edge or end, of the angel's jurisdiction, which may be signified by the very end of the feathers of his wings. The *wings* (Hebrew: *kanaph,* "extremity, edge, flap of a wing, quarter or section of a building, border, corner, uttermost part, feather") *of the wind* (Hebrew: *ruwach,* "wind, breath, spirit, region of the sky, air, gust, tempest") indicates that the angels' presence, power, and authority can be limited to his proximity, and it can be approached or avoided. Realizing this fact, we ought to take the initiative and seek to be where the Lord is coming down, where the heavens are open and His special anointings and distinguished angels are descending freely and graciously.

It can be discerned easily that a certain angel doesn't have authority on the sidewalk just a couple of inches away from the church where he does. It's almost like when a law officer has authority in one city and not in another. Such an angel may be stationed in a particular place and limited to it, but our own angels have jurisdiction over us everywhere we go.

29. Do angels have moods and personal feelings whereby they might become offended? Yes, they do. Gabriel felt insulted when the Priest Zacharias did not believe his report that he would father a child in his old age, (Luke 1:11-20). If I may paraphrase him, he said, "Man, do you realize who I am? I am Gabriel, the one that stands in the very presence of God. It is not a light thing that you should doubt *my* word. Consequently, you shall be mute until the word is fulfilled."

Luke 1:19-20 (tlb) Then the angel said, "I am Gabriel! I stand in the very presence of God. It was He Who sent me to you with this good news! And now, because you haven't believed me, you are to be stricken silent, unable to speak until the child is born. For my words will certainly come true at the proper time."

When an angel appears to a person with an important message from God—especially one of such high authority and distinction as Gabriel, the Chief Messenger of Divine Revelations—it is crucial to receive and not grieve him. The Lord will give us special faith to be able to receive such a visitation, but, insofar as He would allow us to react, interact or respond to him, it behooves us to be quick to listen and agree with him and not to speak in the flesh, (Ecclesiastes 5:6). For not knowing how to cooperate with supernatural manifestations, many people have forfeited a special blessing from the Lord.

On the other hand, the Prophet Daniel was highly favored by the visitation of Gabriel because of his disposition to it.

Daniel 10:7 (tlb) I, Daniel, alone saw this great vision; the men with me saw nothing, but they were suddenly filled with unreasoning terror and ran to hide, and I was left alone. When I saw this frightening vision my strength left me, and I grew pale and weak with fright.

It appears that Gabriel was sent to speak only to Daniel, and that he caused the men that were with him to tremble and flee. But if he was going to speak to all of them (for they were all praying and fasting), he may have become grieved by their unreasoning fear and sudden departure. So when he turned again to see that Daniel was still there, he became glad and very pleased with him and called him a man "greatly beloved," (Daniel 10:11). He even took the liberty to share a lot of important insights about the spiritual realm—including future events—on that occasion, because he felt most comfortable in dialoguing with this man of excellent spirit and so greatly beloved.

Another time that the angels were in a good mood was when Jesus was born. The sense we get from reading the precious story of our Savior's birth is that there was so much joy and celebration in the heavens over this most important event that, unscheduled as it were, the angels simply could not contain themselves and burst out right into the seen realm shouting "Glory! Glory to God...!" (Luke 1:8-14).

Angels can be pleased, and angels can be grieved. As God's mediators, they show God's emotions insofar as they are representatives of him. Each angel is a unique creation of God which represents an attribute of Him. So whether we please or displease God, we have two witnesses—His Spirit within us, and His angels outside us—bearing witness and testifying to us of His feelings about our behavior.

I read an illustrated book about angels and became very impressed by a set of illustrations depicting a variety of moods which angels can exhibit. It showed a little boy taking jam without his mother's permission, and an angel beside him weeping because of it. The sadness, guilt or remorse we feel for having done something wrong can be either the conviction of our own conscience, a check or tug of the Holy Spirit in our hearts, an angel's presence emitting feelings of sadness and displeasure, or any combination of these.

That book also shows an illustration of angels expressing happiness at the sight of children feeding birds kindly. Angels are extremely sensitive and intensely close to us, and when we treat God's creation with respect, especially other people, they are glad. Even in the simplest of our words, motives, thoughts and deeds, the angels are ever-so-near, aware and quick to reflect by their presence.

30. With so much activity of the angels in our lives, some people might think we ought to get to know them on a personal basis, perhaps by name. Can or should we know the names of our angels? How closely can we know, converse and interact with them? With so much mention of the angels in the Bible, there are only two specifically named: Michael and Gabriel. (The Catholic Bible includes Raphael.) Never are we shown how to or encouraged to fellowship or get well acquainted with our angels, but to seek the Lord and to become intimate with Him. Paul said, "That I may win *Christ,* and be found *in Him,* and *know Him,"* (Philippians 3:8-10).

Colossians 1:18-19 (niv) Do not let anyone who delights in false humility and the worship of angels disqualify you for the prize. Such a person goes into great detail about what he has seen, and his unspiritual mind puffs him up with idle notions. He has lost connection with the Head, from Whom the whole Body, supported and held together by its ligaments and sinews, grows as God causes it to grow.

God is able to cause us to grow as we stay firmly connected to Jesus, the Head of the Church. Emphasizing any other being above the Head is always inappropriate, unbiblical and unprofitable. If an angel was to identify himself by name, which rarely occurs, then that's fine. There are, in fact, some valid accounts, in history and now, of individuals that enjoy genuine relationships with angels and know them by name, but this is not the norm, and it should be established by God. Some people are more spiritually disposed, and some are used of God in distinctive ways with regard to angelic activity.

There are also some confused persons that mumble to themselves and try to have dialog with angels that doesn't edify. There are others who try too hard to experience supernaturals, others who try to appear super spiritual, and others who tend—or wish—to mislead by purporting to communicate with angels. I think being sober is best. Just acknowledge them as appropriate and keep the focus on Jesus, the Lord of the angels. You may ask your angel to assist you with matters, (and, in some cases, thank him, as when Gabriel asked me to thank him for assisting me in the writing of my Dreams book), but to request his name or to give him a name, or to attend to or adore him, is a fallacy. We should only know so much detail about our ministering spirits—remember, they are only servants.

According to the Bible, it seems that asking God for their services, receiving messages from them, and invoking their help and assistance is the only kind of acknowledgement that the angels ought to receive from us. We are not encouraged to have conversations with them, however, that's not completely forbidden. The Bible records several instances in which there was dialogue between persons and angels, but they only occurred within the context of a supernatural vision or angelic visitation—which was always temporary and occurred only once or very seldom in one's lifetime. There never was, in Bible times, nor should there be with us now, ongoing casual conversations or small talks on a natural level between angels and people.

We are born-again by faith in *Jesus Christ;* are dead to sin and made alive in *Him;* we are to know *Him,* draw nearer to *Him,* and be hidden in *Him.* And when He returns, we shall return with *Him* in glory, know *Him* even as we are known of Him, and forever discover the unsearchable riches of *Christ. To Whom* be all the glory, honor and praise, and *to Him* be all our energies, focus, time and attention.

Salvation Prayer

John 3:16 **For God so loved the world, that He gave His only begotten Son, that whosoever believeth in Him should not perish, but have everlasting life.**

Romans 10:9-10 **That if thou shalt confess with thy mouth the Lord Jesus, and shalt believe in thine heart that God hath raised Him from the dead, thou shalt be saved. For with the heart man believeth unto righteousness; and with the mouth confession is made unto salvation. For the Scripture saith, Whosoever believeth on Him shall not be ashamed.**

"Oh Lord God, I come to You in the precious Name of Jesus, and repent of my sins. Please have mercy on me, forgive me, and wash me in the Holy Blood of Jesus. I believe that Jesus Christ died for my sins and was raised from the dead for my justification, and I accept Him into my heart right now, to be my personal Lord and Savior. I trust You to take out of my life anything that is not pleasing to You, anything that is not according to Your Holy Word."

"Fill me with the power of Your mighty Holy Spirit, and transform me into the kind of person You want me to be. I'm saved now, through faith in Jesus Christ, I belong to You, Lord God, and I commit myself completely to Your will. I will pray, I will read the Bible, I will go to church, and I will serve You in any and every way You want me to. Have Your way in my life, completely, and use me for Your glory. In the precious Name of Jesus. Amen."

---

sign your name and date here, and as you do so, believe, by faith, that it is also being written in the Lamb's (Jesus) Book of Life in Heaven, (Revelation 20:11-15).

Books by David A. Castro

Understanding Supernatural Dreams According to the Bible
A Living Classic, $24.95

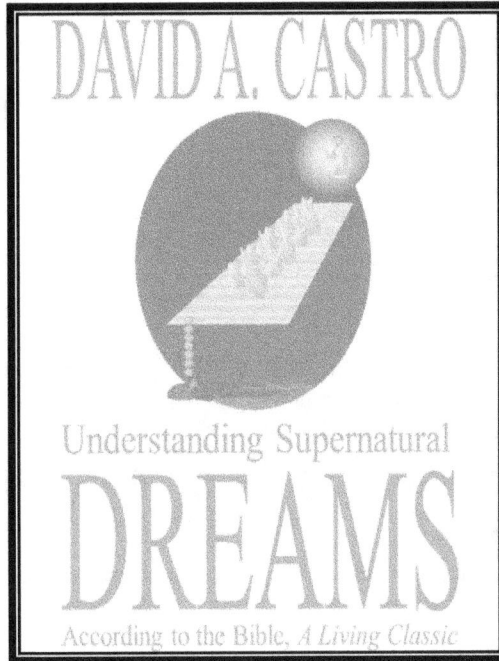

A profoundly spiritual, strictly biblical work, this expository reference book may be considered "required reading" for students of the Spirit. It takes the reader on into the spiritual realm and examines dreams therefrom. A classic in its field, it offers to help the reader understand the broad spectrum of dreams and dreaming, and may assist in healing and deliverance from sleep/dream problems. It provides many practical guidelines on trances, audible voices, out-of-body experiences, and other kinds of visions, and encourages the Body of Christ to yield to the Holy Spirit for supernatural experiences along these lines. Highly Recommended.

Chapters include: What is a Dream?; Be Renewed in the Spirit of Your Dream Life; Sleep in Heavenly Peace; Adventures in the Night Seasons; Dream Recall and Interpretation; Try the Dreams Whether they are of God; Some Experiences; Supernatural Dreams and Trances; Endtime Dreamers; Glossary; 254 pages; 8¼ x 10½"

Understanding Supernatural Visions According to the Bible
$19.95

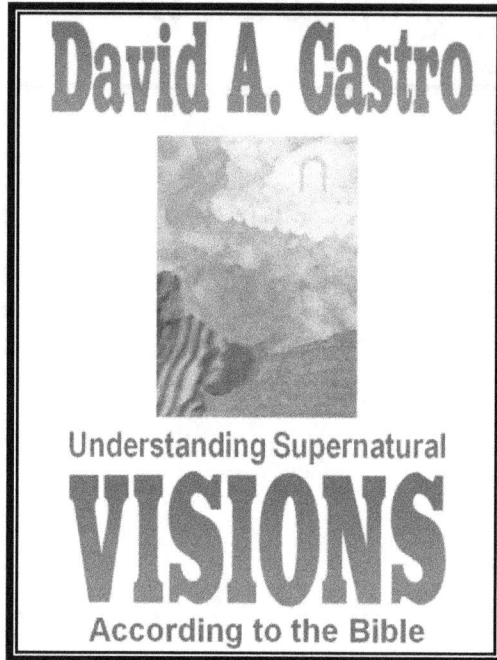

Explores a variety of different kinds of visions and clarifies many issues involved in the various realms of supernatural revelations. It encourages Christians to seek those things which are Above (Colossians 3:1), while at the same time challenges us to gain a foundation in the Word of God, to check the motives of our own hearts, and to walk in the anointing of the Holy Spirit with Jesus. It is profoundly insightful and helpful to prophets, intercessors, and others who receive visions and revelations of the Lord.

Chapters include: Spiritual Vision; Pictorial Vision; Panoramic Vision; Dream (Night Vision); Audible Message; Apparition; Divine Sight; Open Heaven; Trance; Out-of-body Experience; Translation; Heavenly Visitation; Wisdom is the Principal Thing; Glossary; 100 pages; 8¼ x 10½"

Understanding Voices, Noises & Presences
in the Spiritual Realm, $14.95

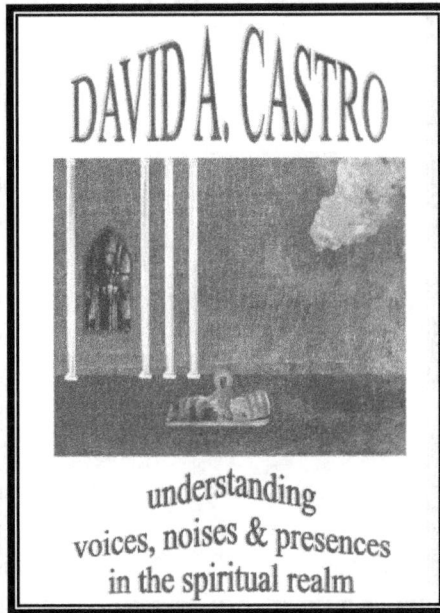

DAVID A. CASTRO

understanding
voices, noises & presences
in the spiritual realm

In this unique booklet, David addresses spiritual and mystical experiences in a refreshingly insightful manner. As always, he teaches strictly from the Bible as he shines new light on the subject of the spiritual realm and its various manifestations. He shows how to discern which experiences are of God, and endeavors to remove fear and impart faith for supernatural experiences which are of Him.

Chapters include: Yield to the Spirit; Peculiar Disclosings; Angelic Involvement; Spiritual Presences Around People; Spiritual Presences in Certain Places; Portals, Pathways and Structures; Ask Wisdom; Prayers; 74 pages; 7 x 10"

The Supernatural Ministry of Angels
$14.95

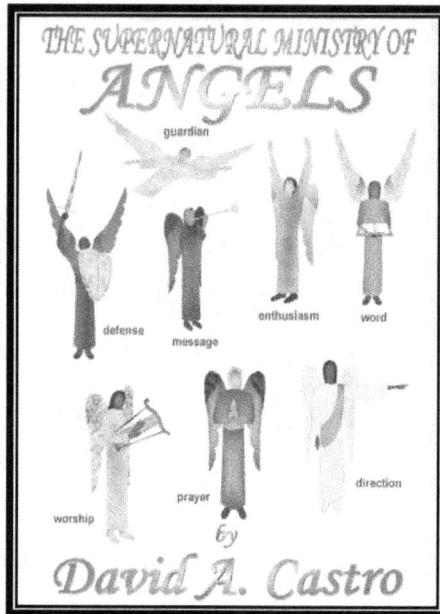

THE SUPERNATURAL MINISTRY OF

ANGELS

guardian

defense

message

enthusiasm

word

worship

prayer

direction

by

David A. Castro

A thorough yet concise study on the ministry of angels according to the Bible. No mythical, fancy ideas or popular notions are given, but a truly scriptural observation and general analysis of the entire spectrum of angels. 30 questions about angels and their personal, practical involvement in our lives are answered, and where the Scripture is silent or unclear, qualified opinion is given.

Chapters include: A Prophecy; Kinds of Angels; Jesus, Lord of Angels; Angelic Fellow-Servants; Angels Unawares; Angelic Providence; Evil Angels; Serving God Releases Angels; Tongues of Angels; 30 Questions & Answers; includes a General Listing of Angelic Orders and Employments; 74 pages; 7 x 10"

Understanding Supernatural Experiences According to the Bible
$24.95

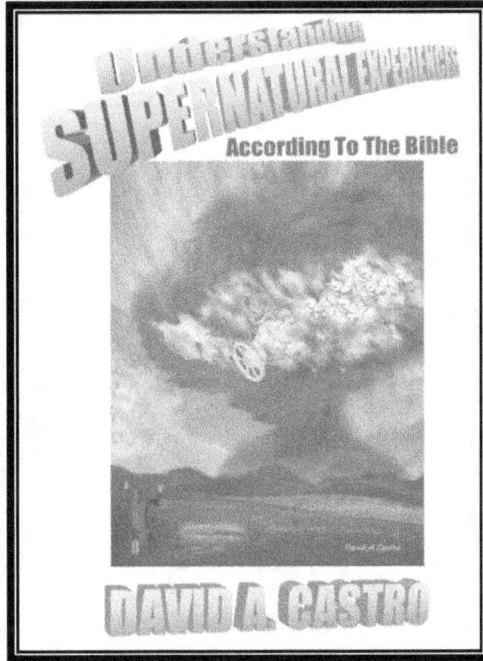

Over twenty years in the making, this extraordinary writing reveals how the supernatural realm works, what the Holy Spirit is able to do, and encourages God's people to embrace the supernatural dimensions of the anointing. Signs and wonders in the heavens and in the earth—revival, special anointings and the Shekinah Glory, trances, stigmata and levitation—are all explained.

Chapters include: Seek the Things Above; My Personal Testimony; The Power of Revelations; Now Concerning Supernaturals; Kinds of Supernatural Experiences; Special Anointings; Understanding the Anointing; Judging Supernatural Experiences; History of Signs and Wonders; Prepare Ye the Way of the Lord; 184 pages; 8¼ x 10½"

30 Years of Dreams Visions Trances
$14.95

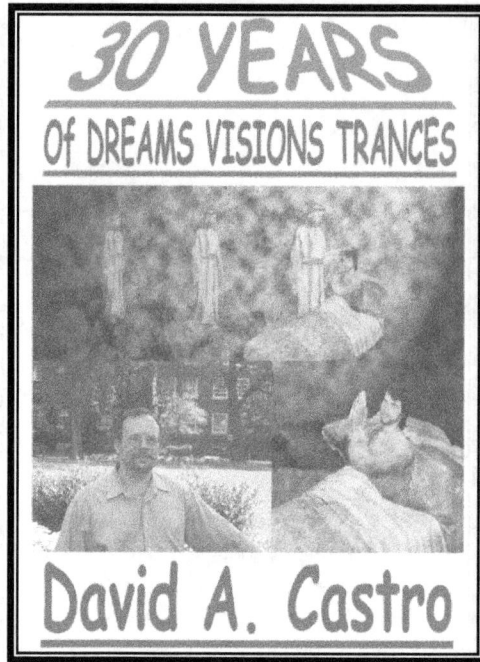

Here David shares a number of supernatural experiences that he has had from the time of his conversion in 1979, in Honolulu, Hawaii. In a wide range of dreams, visions, trances, angelic encounters, and manifestations of the voice of God, he has come to understand their dynamic functions, and hopes to impart wisdom and anointing to the reader through the sharing of the experiences.

Chapters include: Shekinah Glory; Family History; How I Became Christian; I Want to Serve God; How God Speaks in Visions; 74 pages; 7 x 10"

THE SUPERNATURAL MINISTRY OF ANGELS

Please order online from www.Amazon.com

	Order Form Sample		
Qty	Title	Each	Price
	Understanding Supernatural Dreams According to the Bible, *A Living Classic*	$24.95	
	Understanding Supernatural Visions According to the Bible	$19.95	
	Understanding Voices, Noises & Presences in the Spiritual Realm	$14.95	
	The Supernatural Ministry of Angels	$14.95	
	Understanding Supernatural Experiences According to the Bible	$24.95	
	30 Years of Dreams Visions Trances	$14.95	
		SubTotal	
		S & H	
		Total	

THE SUPERNATURAL MINISTRY OF ANGELS

ॐ ॐ

www.brooklynblessing.com

www.twitter.com/daword

www.ingramcontent.com/pod-product-compliance
Lightning Source LLC
LaVergne TN
LVHW061229060426
835509LV00012B/1471